Dedicated to Josh Hathaway.

—M.L.

Copyright © 2021 by Mike Lowery

Special thanks to Dr. Jackie Faherty, Astrophysicist at the American Museum of Natural History, for her guidance and expert verification of the information included in this book.

Library of Congress Cataloging-in-Publication Data available
ISBN 978-1-338-35974-9
10 9 8 7 6 5 4 3 2 1   21 22 23 24 25
Printed in China   62 • First edition, September 2021
The text type was set in Gotham.
The display type was hand lettered by Mike Lowery.
Book design by Doan Buu

EVERYTHING AWESOME ABOUT SPACE AND OTHER GALACTIC FACTS

WRITTEN AND ILLUSTRATED BY

MIKE LOWERY

Orchard Books
New York
An Imprint of Scholastic Inc.

OH, HELLO.

I'M (MIKE LOWERY)

AND I'D LIKE to SHOW YOU SOMETHING.

IT'S A **GIANT BOOK ABOUT SPACE!**

(YOU'RE HOLDING IT RIGHT NOW!)

IT'S **TOTALLY** (LOADED) WITH **INFO,** (WEIRD) **FACTS,** AND **JOKES** THAT ARE **OUT OF THIS WORLD!**

SPACE IS AWESOME AND IT'S FULL OF SOME PRETTY AMAZING THINGS!

INSIDE YOU'LL LEARN ABOUT:

EXPLODING STARS!

WEIRD SPACE FOOD!

ROCKETS!

AND LOTS MORE!

THANKS FOR TAKING A LOOK! - MIKE

TABLE of CONTENTS

PART ONE

THE UNIVERSE

(AKA EVERYTHING!)

WELCOME TO

SPACE!

WAIT, WHAT (IS) SPACE?!

Well, SPACE (also called "outer space") is anything outside planet Earth where we live. There's no exact spot away from the surface of Earth where outer space starts, but the Kármán line is often used. It is a marker 62 miles above Earth's average sea level.

THE KÁRMÁN LINE

THE UNIVERSE IS EVERYTHING THAT EXISTS.

The universe contains asteroids, planets, black holes, galaxies, and even YOU. The universe is EVERYTHING.

THE COSMOS

Sometimes we also call it the "cosmos." The words cosmos and universe can both be used! The only difference is that "cosmos" is a word we use to imply that there is a harmonious order to everything (instead of just chaos!).

Space, outer space, the cosmos... whatever you want to call it ... it's BIG. I mean it's REALLY BIG.

Because things are so spread out and far away from us in the cosmos, we don't measure the distance in inches or feet. We would have to deal with so many looonnnggg numbers, so scientists have simplified things for us. Instead, we use...

LIGHT- YEARS

ZOOOM!

Nothing travels faster than light (that we know of). It travels 670 million miles per hour, and over 180,000 miles per second. That's fast enough to go around Earth more than SEVEN TIMES every second.

A light-year is how far light would travel in one year. That's about 5.8 trillion miles! In fact, it's:

5,869,713,600,000 MILES

(9,446,388,363,878 kilometers).

HERE ARE JUST A FEW EXAMPLES OF HOW FAR AWAY OBJECTS IN SPACE ARE:

HI!

THE SUN
8 LIGHT-MINUTES
(93.2 MILLION MILES)

THE NEAREST STAR,
PROXIMA CENTAURI
(4.2 LIGHT-YEARS)

THE NEAREST LARGE-SPIRAL GALAXY,
ANDROMEDA
(2.5 MILLION LIGHT-YEARS)

AND THE FARTHEST GALAXIES THAT CAN BE SEEN IN THE UNIVERSE ARE **TENS OF BILLIONS** OF LIGHT-YEARS AWAY!

KA-BOOM!

We don't know how big the universe is exactly, but we do know that it's

GETTING BIGGER!

We know this because astronomers have observed faraway galaxies moving away from us through space. In 1927, a Belgian priest and astronomer named Georges Lemaître is one of the scientists who came up with a theory that the universe began in one small spot and started moving apart quickly after a big explosion! We call this . . .

THE BIG BANG!

HOW OLD IS THE UNIVERSE?

Cosmologists (scientists who study the beginning and evolution of the universe) believe that the big bang happened around **13.8 BILLION YEARS AGO.**

WEIRD FACT!

Most of the hydrogen atoms in your body were formed during the big bang.

THE UNIVERSE IS MADE UP OF TWO THINGS:

MATTER (AND) ENERGY

Matter is all of the things that we can see, like stars and planets, but it also Includes something called

DARK MATTER.

We can't see dark matter, but we know it's there because scientists can observe how visible matter interacts with it.

Energy is all of the light and radiation in the universe. There is also an unknown force that scientists call

DARK ENERGY.

We think dark energy is also what is making the universe expand.

DARK ENERGY MAKES UP ABOUT 68% OF THE KNOWN UNIVERSE!

TOTALLY INVISIBLE

WEIRD FACT!

The universe is mostly made up of dark energy and dark matter that we can't see at all . . . and that we have a hard time understanding. Planets, stars, and galaxies only make up roughly 4–5%. Everything else is totally invisible!

SPEAKING OF INVISIBLE, LET'S TALK ABOUT... GRAVITY.

Gravity is a force that pulls objects toward each other. It's not something we can see with our eyes, but we can see the effects of it. The heavier the object, the more PULL it has. Everything with mass has gravity, even YOU! (But we are very small objects compared to planets, so our gravitational pull is so small it's not noticeable.)

Gravity is important because it's what holds galaxies together, it makes our planets orbit around the Sun, and it's what keeps you from flying off into space! The center of Earth is pulling us toward it and has just the right amount of pull so we don't get squished and so we don't float.

Our star, the Sun, has a lot of gravity, and it's pulling the planets toward it. Luckily, our orbit keeps us at just the right distance from the Sun so we don't get too hot or too cold.

NEBULAS

THERE ARE GIANT CLOUDS OF GASES AND DUST IN SPACE CALLED NEBULAS! THE GAS AND DUST CAN BE FROM STARS THAT HAVE EXPLODED, BUT ALSO CAN BE FROM AREAS WHERE STARS ARE FORMED. THESE STAR-MAKING NEBULAS ARE CALLED "STAR NURSERIES."

NEBULAS
FLOAT AROUND IN SPACE BETWEEN STARS: ONE OF THE CLOSEST TO US IS 700 LIGHT-YEARS AWAY.

THERE'S ONE NAMED THE HELIX NEBULA THAT LOOKS LIKE A BIG, SPOOKY EYE!

SHHHHH! SPACE IS TOTALLY SILENT! SOUND WAVES CAN'T TRAVEL IN SPACE BECAUSE IT'S A BIG VACUUM.

GALAXIES

GALAXIES ARE COLLECTIONS OF STARS, PLANETS, GAS, AND OTHER CELESTIAL OBJECTS HELD TOGETHER BY GRAVITY FLOATING THROUGH SPACE.

GALAXIES COME IN DIFFERENT SHAPES:

SPIRAL

ELLIPTICAL

IRREGULAR

WE DIDN'T KNOW OTHER GALAXIES EXISTED UNTIL 1923!

EDWIN HUBBLE
(astronomer)

observed a star that's now called Hubble variable number 1 (or just V1). He was able to calculate how far away it was by observing its patterns of brightness. Turns out, it was farther away than any star in our galaxy! It belongs to a neighboring galaxy, Andromeda.

OUR GALAXY
THE MILKY WAY

SOMETIMES AT NIGHT IF THE CONDITIONS ARE JUST RIGHT, IT'S ACTUALLY POSSIBLE TO SEE THE MILKY WAY IN THE SKY. IT SORT OF LOOKS LIKE A RIVER OF STARS MADE OF FAINT LIGHT. THAT LIGHT IS COMING FROM OTHER STARS IN THE GALAXY.

Lucky for us, our galaxy is in a relatively quiet part of the universe. But it's not standing still. It's actually traveling through space at a speed of 1.3 million miles per hour!

THE MILKY WAY IS THOUGHT TO BE A BARRED SPIRAL-SHAPED GALAXY.

100,000 LIGHT-YEARS WIDE!

LONG AGO, THE GREEKS CALLED IT "GALAXIAS KYKLOS," WHICH MEANS "MILKY CIRCLE," AND THE ROMANS CALLED IT "VIA LACTEA," WHICH MEANS "ROAD OF MILK."

AT THE CENTER IS A SUPER-MASSIVE BLACK HOLE!

AROUND 7 NEW STARS ARE FORMED EVERY YEAR IN OUR GALAXY!

HEY!

WATCH IT!

Sometimes galaxies will collide when they're passing each other. When they do, thousands (or more!) new stars are born.

Some small galaxies have even crashed into our galaxy. Ten billion years ago, the Milky Way collided with a dwarf galaxy that had a strange name, "the Gaia Sausage" (also known as "Gaia-Enceladus").

And it looks like the Milky Way will crash again! Don't worry, a big collision won't happen again for a few billion years!

Floating in our galaxy is a GIANT, likely planet-sized DIAMOND. It's actually the heart of an old star. Its real name is "BPM 37093," but astronomers call it "Lucy" after the Beatles' song "Lucy in the Sky with Diamonds."

PART TWO

THE SOLAR SYSTEM

THIS IS OUR SOLAR SYSTEM.

Well, sort of. The planets aren't really this close together. It's drawn this way so you could see the planets in order, but the planets are way farther apart from each other than they look here. There's no way you could fit an accurate image of the distance between the planets in a book and get the scale right.

THE SUN

JUPITER

EARTH

MERCURY

MARS

VENUS

ASTEROID BELT

MOST OF THE SOLAR SYSTEM IS JUST EMPTY SPACE!

IF YOU MADE A SCALE MODEL OF THE SOLAR SYSTEM WHERE EARTH WAS THE SIZE OF A MARBLE, THE MODEL WOULD BE **7 MILES LONG!**

SATURN

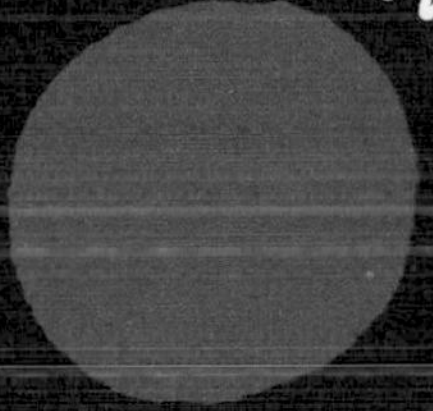

NEPTUNE

COMET

URANUS

PLUTO (DWARF PLANET)

At the center of our solar system is a giant, fiery star called the Sun. The gravitational pull from the Sun causes eight planets (and a dwarf planet called Pluto) to orbit around it, but the planets aren't the only celestial objects in our solar system.

A PLANET'S ORBIT IS THE PATH IT TAKES ROTATING AROUND THE SUN.

THE SUN

The Sun is really important to life on Earth. In fact, it's the most important thing in our solar system. The light and heat that come from the Sun are what make life on Earth possible.

IT'S THE CENTER OF OUR SOLAR SYSTEM!

MADE OF MOSTLY HYDROGEN AND HELIUM
↓

MOST IMPORTANT THING IN OUR SOLAR SYSTEM

#1

AWARD

One day the Sun will burn out and collapse. Then it will be about the size of Earth. But don't worry, that's not for another 5–7 billion years.

YOU COULD FIT ONE MILLION EARTHS INSIDE OF THE SUN.

And yet, the Sun is really only a medium-sized star. There's a star called Betelgeuse (pronounced "Beetle Juice") whose radius is 700 times bigger!

Many ancient cultures worshipped the Sun! Ra (or Re) was the Sun god in ancient Egypt and was often considered to be the king of all other gods.

LIGHT TAKES ABOUT 8 MINUTES TO GET FROM THE SUN TO EARTH!

I'M MELLLTINNGG!

THE SURFACE OF THE SUN IS HOT ENOUGH TO MAKE DIAMONDS BOIL!

ARE WE THERE YET?!

IF YOU COULD FLY IN A REGULAR AIRPLANE TO THE SUN, IT WOULD TAKE 20 YEARS TO GET THERE!

The Sun makes up 99.8% of all the mass in our solar system.

THE PLANETS

1. MERCURY

(38.592 MILLION MILES FROM THE SUN)

- -

★ THE CLOSEST PLANET TO THE SUN!

★ ONE DAY ON MERCURY IS 1,408 EARTH HOURS!

★ SUPER HOT DURING THE DAY AND FREEZING AT NIGHT!

(EVEN THOUGH MERCURY IS THE CLOSEST PLANET TO THE SUN, VENUS IS HOTTER.)

HAS NO ATMOSPHERE ↓

4 BILLION YEARS AGO, A HUUUUGE ASTEROID SMASHED INTO IT AND LEFT A CRATER THE SIZE OF TEXAS!

TAKES 88 DAYS TO ORBIT THE SUN

COVERED IN IMPACT CRATERS FROM COMETS AND ASTEROIDS

NAMED AFTER THE GREEK GOD HERMES, WHO WAS VERY FAST. THIS IS BECAUSE MERCURY ORBITS THE SUN VERY QUICKLY.

IT'S ALMOST THE SAME SIZE AS EARTH.

BECAUSE IT'S SO CLOSE TO EARTH, IT IS THE THIRD-BRIGHTEST NATURAL OBJECT WE CAN SEE IN THE NIGHT SKY. (THE MOON AND THE SUN ARE BRIGHTER!)

ONE DAY ON VENUS IS 243 EARTH DAYS.

IT SPINS IN THE OPPOSITE DIRECTION FROM THE OTHER PLANETS.

VENUS HAS A THICK ATMOSPHERE THAT TRAPS HEAT. ITS AVERAGE TEMPERATURE IS 863 DEGREES.

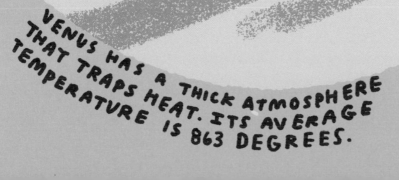

HOTTEST PLANET AWARD

3. EARTH

(93.281 MILLION MILES FROM THE SUN)

4.54 BILLION YEARS OLD

REVOLVES AROUND THE SUN AT **67,000** MILES PER HOUR!

BEST PLANET AWARD

HAS ICY POLES

WATER COVERS **2/3** OF THE EARTH'S SURFACE.

EARTH IS AN INCREDIBLY SPECIAL PLANET.

WHY? → IT'S WHERE YOU LIVE.

IT'S THE ONLY PLANET WHERE LIFE HAS BEEN DISCOVERED!

IT'S THE ONLY PLANET TO HAVE MASSIVE OCEANS OF LIQUID WATER, WHERE LIFE BEGAN.

IT'S JUST THE RIGHT DISTANCE FROM THE SUN.

JUST RIGHT.

IT'S NOT TOO HOT OR COLD!

ONE YEAR IS ACTUALLY 365.26 DAYS.

THIS IS WHY WE HAVE LEAP YEARS! EVERY FOUR YEARS THERE IS AN EXTRA DAY AT THE END OF FEBRUARY.

IT ROTATES AT A 23.50 TILT.

THIS IS WHAT CAUSES THE SEASONS.

EARTH'S

OKAY, SO IT'S NOT A PLANET BUT IT'S PRETTY IMPORTANT!

LOTS OF PLANETS HAVE MOONS.

BUT MINE IS THE **BEST**!

12 PEOPLE HAVE WALKED ON IT.

OUCH!

Some astronomers believe that the Moon was formed billions of years ago when a planet the size of Mars crashed into Earth. The smaller planet was destroyed and some of the leftover pieces later formed together with pieces of earth and made the Moon.

MOONQUAKES!

THE MOON HAS QUAKES, A LOT LIKE EARTHQUAKES. THEY CAN LAST UP TO HALF AN HOUR. (MOST EARTHQUAKES LAST JUST A FEW SECONDS.)

KA-BOOM!

The United States almost detonated a nuclear bomb on the Moon in the 1950s! After the Soviet satellite Sputnik was launched and was a huge success, the United States wanted to show off a little, too. So, they had the idea to send a bomb to the Moon! Luckily, they decided not to because they were worried about raising radiation levels, which could have hurt further Moon missions.

WAIT, WHAT ?!

MOON

You would be much lighter on the Moon! The Moon has only 1/6 the gravity of Earth, so if you weigh 100 pounds on Earth, you'd weigh about 16.6 pounds on the Moon.

ITS GRAVITY IS LARGELY THE REASON THE OCEAN HAS TIDES.

IT'S SLOWLY MOVING AWAY FROM EARTH (LESS THAN 1.5 INCHES A YEAR)!

¼ THE SIZE OF EARTH

FIFTH-BIGGEST MOON IN THE SOLAR SYSTEM

JOIN THE DARK SIDE!

One side of the Moon is constantly facing away from Earth, which caused some to call this the "dark side" of the Moon. This is totally inaccurate! It actually gets a lot of light, so astronomers call it the "far side" of the Moon.

ICE HAS BEEN FOUND UNDER THE SURFACE.

ECLIPSES!

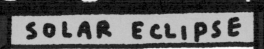

SOLAR ECLIPSE

When the Moon is aligned perfectly between Earth and the Sun, the Moon will obstruct our view, creating a solar eclipse. This happens roughly twice a year, but you have to be in the right spot on Earth to see them.

LUNAR ECLIPSE

When Earth is directly between the Sun and the Moon, Earth blocks the light that is hitting the Moon, causing it to look very faint. During a lunar eclipse the Moon's temperature can drop dramatically. In 10–30 minutes it can drop to -280 degrees Fahrenheit!

72,000 FEET TALL

OLYMPUS MONS

29,029 FEET TALL

MOUNT EVEREST

MARS HAS A MOUNTAIN CALLED **OLYMPUS MONS** AND IT'S THE BIGGEST MOUNTAIN IN THE ENTIRE SOLAR SYSTEM!

IT'S OVER **13** MILES TALL!

THAT'S MORE THAN TWICE THE HEIGHT OF MT. EVEREST.

HAS TWO REALLY SMALL MOONS

←PHOBOS
AND
←DEIMOS

HAS REALLY BAD DUST STORMS THAT CAN LAST FOR MONTHS!

HELLO? ANYBODY HOME?

VIKINGS IN SPACE!

We've had lots of uncrewed missions to Mars. The first from NASA was the Viking probe. The probe was made up of two parts, an orbiter and a lander. The orbiter circled Mars while taking photos, and the lander made observations from the surface. They found dried-up rivers and other signs that it probably once rained on Mars!

5. JUPITER

(484 MILLION MILES FROM THE SUN)

IT'S **HUGE!** NOT ONLY IS IT THE BIGGEST PLANET IN THE SOLAR SYSTEM, IT'S MORE THAN **TWO AND A HALF TIMES** THE MASS OF ALL OF THE OTHER PLANETS COMBINED!

SPINS FASTER THAN THE OTHER PLANETS

HAS VERY FAINT RINGS MADE UP OF SMALL DUST PARTICLES

A REALLY BIG MOON!

IT HAS AT LEAST 79 MOONS, INCLUDING GANYMEDE, THE BIGGEST ONE IN THE SOLAR SYSTEM. IT'S BIGGER THAN MERCURY AND PLUTO!

Jupiter doesn't have a solid surface like Earth does—it's just stacked layers of gases, so you wouldn't be able to walk on it.

BIGGEST PLANET IN OUR SOLAR SYSTEM AWARD!

Its center is a mystery to astronomers. Some think that maybe the core is either a hot liquid or possibly a solid rock fourteen times the size of Earth.

IT'S REALLY **BRIGHT!** YOU CAN SEE IT IN THE NIGHT SKY WITHOUT A TELESCOPE.

It's the fourth-brightest thing in the sky after the Sun, Moon, and Venus.

THE GREAT RED SPOT

On the surface of Jupiter is a storm that never stops, and it's 1.3 times the size of Earth. Winds in the Great Red Spot can travel twice as fast as the most powerful hurricanes on Earth.

6. SATURN

(930 MILLION MILES FROM THE SUN)

LIKE JUPITER, IT'S BRIGHT ENOUGH TO SEE AT NIGHT WITHOUT A TELESCOPE.

MY TEACHER SAYS I'M VERY BRIGHT.

It's another giant, gassy planet!

It's made up of mostly hydrogen and helium. If you tried to fly through it, you wouldn't be able to land, and the very high pressure and temperatures would... um... not be very good for your spaceship!

HAS A MOON BIGGER THAN THE PLANET MERCURY!

MOST MOONS AWARD

HAS AT LEAST

53 MOONS

(53 ARE CONFIRMED, WHILE AT LEAST 29 ARE WAITING TO BE!)

THAT'S MORE THAN ANY OTHER PLANET IN THE SOLAR SYSTEM.

HAS RINGS MADE OF PARTICLES OF **ICE** AND **ROCK** ↘

ITS RINGS ARE **THOUSANDS** OF MILES **WIDE,** BUT (IN MOST PLACES) ONLY ABOUT 30 **FEET TALL.**

Saturn's E ring is 600,000 miles wide!

ABOUT **9 TIMES WIDER** THAN **EARTH**

BEST **RINGS** AWARD!

7. URANUS

(1.841 BILLION MILES FROM THE SUN)

ICE GIANT

MOST OF URANUS'S MASS IS MADE UP OF:
- SUPER-COLD WATER
- METHANE
- AMMONIA

DRESS WARM!

IF YOU WANT TO GO TO URANUS, YOU SHOULD BRING A COAT!

COLDEST PLANET AWARD!

It has the coldest atmosphere of any planet in our solar system! It can get as cold as -360 degrees!

ROTATES AT A 97.8° ANGLE!

(which means it rotates on its side)

ON EARTH, SEASONS LAST JUST A FEW MONTHS. ON URANUS, SEASONS LAST

42 YEARS!

IT GETS ITS BLUEISH-GREEN COLOR FROM ALL OF THE METHANE GAS IN ITS ATMOSPHERE.

HAS VERY SMALL RINGS MADE UP OF ROCKS AND DUST.

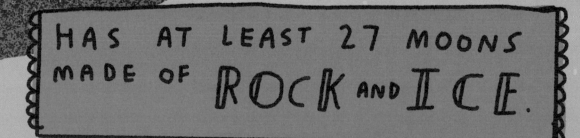

HAS AT LEAST 27 MOONS MADE OF ROCK AND ICE.

TAKES 84 YEARS TO GO AROUND THE SUN.

8. NEPTUNE

(2.78 BILLION MILES FROM THE SUN)

THE FARTHEST PLANET (IN OUR SOLAR SYSTEM) FROM THE SUN

HAS 5 VERY THIN RINGS MADE UP OF DUST AND SMALL ROCKS. EACH RING IS NAMED AFTER A FAMOUS ASTRONOMER: GALLE, LE VERRIER, LASSELL, ARAGO, AND ADAMS.

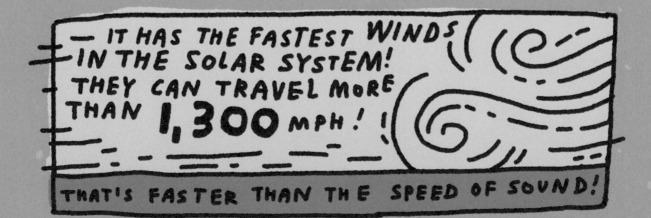

— IT HAS THE FASTEST WINDS IN THE SOLAR SYSTEM! THEY CAN TRAVEL MORE THAN **1,300** MPH!

THAT'S FASTER THAN THE SPEED OF SOUND!

It has fourteen moons.

DISCOVERED IN 1846. ↓

AT ONE TIME, IT HAD A LARGE, FIVE-YEAR STORM, LIKE JUPITER'S RED SPOT, THAT WAS THE SIZE OF EARTH! IT WAS CALLED THE "GREAT DARK SPOT."

IT ALSO HAS A SMALLER STORM CALLED THE "SMALL DARK SPOT"! IT'S NOT REALLY THAT SMALL. IT'S THE SIZE OF EARTH'S MOON!

It has a huge moon named Triton that orbits in the opposite direction of Neptune's rotation! It's the only large moon in our solar system that does this.

ONE YEAR ON NEPTUNE IS 165 EARTH YEARS.

WAIT, WHAT ABOUT PLUTO?!

IN 1930, A GREAT BIG CHUNK OF ICE AND ROCK WAS DISCOVERED ORBITING THE SUN PAST NEPTUNE, AND PLUTO BECAME OUR NINTH PLANET.

NOT A PLANET

AW, MAN.

ACTUALLY A DWARF PLANET

HOWEVER

In 2006, the International Astronomical Union met and made a very tough decision. Since there are many planet-sized objects in the Kuiper Belt and elsewhere in the solar system, they revisited the definition of what actually classified as a planet. So, they made the decision (that some folks didn't exactly LOVE) to define a planet as a celestial body that:

☑ HAS TO ORBIT A STAR. (Pluto orbits the Sun...so, check!)

☑ IS BIG ENOUGH THAT IT BECOMES ROUND FROM ITS OWN GRAVITY. (Yep!)

☒ HAS ENOUGH GRAVITATIONAL PULL THAT IT CLEARS THE AREA AROUND IT.
(This is called "clearing the neighborhood," and it's part of the checklist that Pluto doesn't meet. Pluto is too small to get the objects around it to orbit it, so it's considered a dwarf planet.)

WEIRD FACT!

Pluto has a really weird orbit!
Sometimes it's actually closer to the Sun than Neptune.

ASTEROID BELT

Between the orbits of Mars and Jupiter is the first of two major rocky highways. Most of the objects in the asteroid belt are small, but it's home to a dwarf planet named Ceres. There are also three major asteroids found there: Vesta, Pallas, and Hygiea.

DISCOVERED IN 1801

It was once believed that the belt was made up of bits of a planet that was destroyed a long time ago, but astronomers now know this isn't true.

There are a few companies that want to mine asteroids for things like gold, silver, and platinum.

IT'S NOT AS DENSE AS YOU MIGHT THINK. IF YOU BALLED UP ALL OF THE ROCKS IN THE BELT INTO A BIG BALL, IT WOULD BE ABOUT 96% SMALLER THAN THE MOON!

There is on average 620,000–1.8 million miles between each asteroid.

KUIPER BELT (KY-PER)

Out past Neptune is a ring of icy rocks that revolve around the Sun. It is somewhere between 20 and 200 times the size of the asteroid belt! There are even a few dwarf planets here, like Pluto (sound familiar?), Haumea, and Makemake.

In 1992, the first object in the Kuiper Belt was spotted. It was nicknamed "Smiley" but was later renamed "1992 QB1."

WEIRD FACTS

BONUS

MORE THAN 550 PEOPLE HAVE BEEN TO SPACE!

ASTRONAUT CHRIS HADFIELD SAYS THAT SPACE SMELLS LIKE BURNT STEAK!

Have you ever wondered how many people are in space right now? Well, there's a website that will tell you how many people are in space right now. It's called:
www.howmanypeopleareinspacerightnow.com

PART THREE

THE STARS

WHAT IS A STAR?!

STARS ARE GIANT BALLS OF BURNING GAS!

They can produce a LOT of energy. That's why they're so bright. We have one in our solar system (It's called the SUN ... maybe you've heard of it?!).

IT'S ESTIMATED THAT THE MILKY WAY ALONE HAS APPROXIMATELY 100–400 BILLION STARS!

FROM ANY ONE SPOT ON EARTH YOU CAN SEE AROUND 2,000 STARS!

(on a clear night without a lot of light pollution around).

HOW MANY STARS ARE OUT THERE? WE DON'T KNOW, BUT ONE CALCULATED GUESS IS AT LEAST A SEPTILLION! THAT'S A ONE WITH 24 ZEROS!

1,000,000,000,000,000,000,000,000 !

TRY THIS!

Turn off any bright lights and sit outside and look at the sky. To see more stars at night you need to let your eyes adjust for around 30 minutes. The longer you're in the dark, the better your eyes get at seeing the little specks of light in the night sky.

TWINKLE TWINKLE!

Stars "twinkle" because we are looking at them through Earth's atmosphere. The light coming from the star will bounce and reflect, causing it to appear to turn on and off. This is why telescopes, like the Hubble Space Telescope, are important because they can view stars without having to go through Earth's atmosphere. Planets in our solar system don't "twinkle" like this, because they're much closer than faraway stars.

TYPES OF STARS
DWARF STARS

Most stars are dwarf stars, the smallest and dimmest stars. Our Sun is a dwarf star, but there are stars that are smaller than our Sun.

YELLOW DWARF

Yellow dwarf—like our Sun! Medium-sized stars. These will live for around 10 billion years. Some yellow dwarf stars are actually white. In fact, the Sun is white but looks yellow because we see it through Earth's atmosphere.

WHITE DWARF

When dwarf stars near the end of their life, they've burned up most of their hydrogen, and just the hot core of the star remains. (They can be about the size of Earth.)

RED DWARF

These are the most common types of stars, but they're dim and hard to see without a telescope. Proxima Centauri is the closest star to the Sun, and it's a red dwarf. They live longer than other types of stars, because they burn up their supply of hydrogen more slowly. They can live up to trillions of years.

GIANT STARS

GIANT STARS CAN BE HUNDREDS OF TIMES BIGGER THAN THE SUN.

SUPER GIANT STARS!

THERE ARE STARS THAT ARE 2,000 TIMES THE RADIUS OF OUR SUN AND A BILLION TIMES BRIGHTER!

They're so big and so bright that they burn out quickly, and don't live very long. Some can live to be 30 million years old, while others are only around for a few hundred thousand years.

A STAR IS BORN!

STAR NEBULAS

A NEBULA IS A HUGE SPACE CLOUD FULL OF HYDROGEN GAS AND DUST. ONE TYPE OF NEBULA IS CALLED A STAR NURSERY BECAUSE THIS IS WHERE STARS ARE BORN!

In some spots in the nebula, gases clumps together.

These clouds become dense, and their gravitational pull starts to draw in more gas. It starts to get denser and hotter, and eventually collapses under its own weight and turns into what scientists call a PROTOSTAR.

If it collects enough mass, it can shoot out two giant fountains of gas from the top and bottom!

Eventually, the core gets hot enough to fuse hydrogen and helium, and we officially have a star!

But you'll have to be patient. This process takes millions of years!

SIDE FACT!

There are stars that spin rapidly and shoot out beams of radiation!

They're called Pulsars and were co-discovered by student Jocelyn Bell Burnell when she was studying at Cambridge University. Her research won a Nobel prize—for her professor! Fifty years later, she was awarded the Special Breakthrough Prize in Fundamental Physics, which comes with a check for three million dollars!

CONSTELLATIONS

HUMANS HAVE BEEN LOOKING AT THE STARS SINCE WE'VE BEEN ON THE PLANET.

There are 10,000-year-old cave paintings that show star orientations we can still see today.

ANCIENT SAILORS USED THE STARS LIKE ANCIENT ROAD MAPS FOR CENTURIES. THEY USED THE BRIGHTEST ONES TO HELP THEM FIGURE OUT WHERE THEY WERE.

Polaris is commonly called the "North Star" because the Earth's northern axis is pointed at it almost all year round. If you ever decide to go to the North Pole for an adventure, don't forget to look up. Polaris would be directly over you in the sky. But, the North Star isn't the brightest star in the sky. That title belongs to Sirius A, also known as the "dog star."

CONNECT THE DOTS!

Centuries ago we started assigning shapes to some groupings of stars and formed them into people, animals, and mythological creatures. These groups of stars are called constellations.

There are eighty-eight official constellations. Here are just a few.

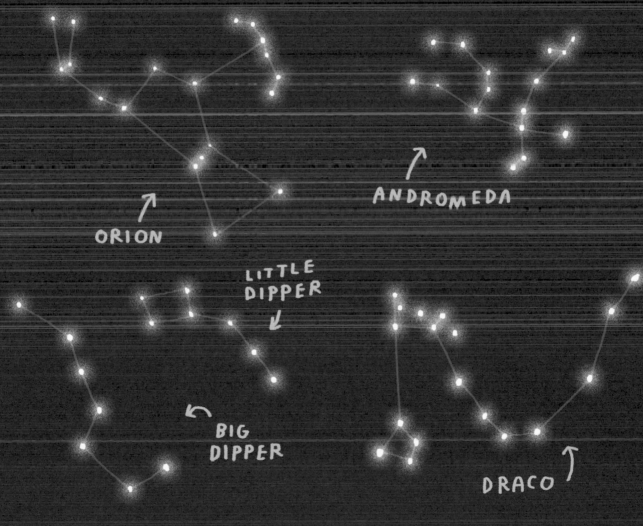

ORION

ANDROMEDA

LITTLE DIPPER

BIG DIPPER

DRACO

The earliest records of these are 3,000 years old, from ancient Babylon (which is where Iraq is today), but we think assigning shapes to star clusters started much earlier than that.

WATCH OUT FOR EXPLODING STARS!

SUPERNOVAS

At the end of its life, giant stars like to go out with a bang! A supernova is what happens when a massive star runs out of fuel.

One way that a supernova happens is by collapsing. These stars create an incredible amount of energy, and the center of the star gets very hot. It then basically can't take the pressure of its own gravity and collapses. The collapse happens so fast that, BOOM, the star explodes.

These supernovas typically happen within a galaxy only two or three times every 100 years.

What it leaves behind depends on how big it was. One option is a dense core, which is called a neutron star. This object can have a radius only a few miles wide but a mass bigger than the Sun's!

You've heard of these strange things in our universe, but are they real? What are they?!

BLACK

When the most massive stars die, what gets left behind is something that is incredibly small in size... but is so dense that nothing can escape it... not even light. It sucks in everything around it.

Sounds spooky, right? Well, what if I told you we are actually

ORBITING A BLACK HOLE!

It's true! Our galaxy has a supermassive black hole in the middle of it! But there's no need to worry. It's 27,000 light years away, so there's not much chance of us getting sucked in.

OUR SUN IS TOO SMALL TO MAKE ONE WHEN IT DIES.

THERE ARE A LOT OF BLACK HOLES. (TOO MANY TO COUNT!)

HOLES!

There are two general categories of black holes. Stellar-mass black holes have just one star. Supermassive black holes have the mass of millions of stars.

EVENT HORIZON

THIS IS THE AREA THAT CAN FORM AROUND THE EDGE OF A BLACK HOLE THAT MARKS THE CLOSEST YOU CAN GET BEFORE GETTING PULLED IN!

SPAGHETTIFICATION?!

Now, look. I know there are a lot of fun facts and jokes in this book, so I understand if you think SPAGHETTIFICATION isn't a real word. BUT IT IS. This is the term that scientists use to describe what would happen to an object if it crossed the event horizon. The gravity is so intense, it would put the part of the object that crosses over into a long, thin shape . . . any idea what it would resemble? Yep! Spaghetti. It's also sometimes called (again, I'm not making this up) "The Noodle Effect."

LOTS OF STARS!

THERE ARE MORE STARS THAN...

ALL OF THE GRAINS OF SAND ON EARTH!

REALLY?!

ALL OF THE WORDS EVER SPOKEN BY HUMANS!

BLAH BLAH BLAH
BLAH BLAH
BLAH BLAH
BLAH BLAH
BLAH BLAH
BLAH BLAH
BLAH BLAH BLAH

ALL OF THE SECONDS THAT HAVE PASSED IN THE 4.5 BILLION YEARS SINCE THE EARTH WAS FORMED!

NO WAY!

SPACE ROCKS
IDENTIFICATION GUIDE

THERE ARE LOTS OF ROCKS FLOATING AROUND IN SPACE. IN FACT, THERE ARE BILLIONS (POSSIBLY TRILLIONS) ORBITING THE SUN.

COMET

A solid chunk of rock, ice, and gas. When a comet passes near the Sun, it starts to melt and begins to release its gases and can produce a glowing exterior and a "tail." Comets gradually get smaller every time they pass by the Sun.

ASTEROID

A large, rocky celestial object left over from the beginning of our solar system. Asteroids can range from as small as 33 feet across to 329 miles across! Most asteroids in our solar system are located in the asteroid belt between Mars and Jupiter. Some may even have water, but probably can't support life as we know it.

← SOME HAVE RINGS!

SOME HAVE MOONS!

METEOROID

Like an asteroid, but smaller.

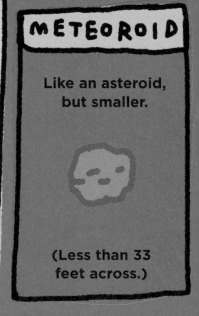

(Less than 33 feet across.)

METEOR

(AKA a shooting star!)

A meteoroid that enters Earth's atmosphere.

METEOR SHOWER

An event when multiple meteors come from the same spot.

WOW!

METEORITE

Any piece of an object that was orbiting in space (like an asteroid or comet) that makes its way through the earth's atmosphere.

OUCH!

BOLIDE

A large meteor that explodes when it enters the atmosphere.

HALLEY'S

CAN BE SEEN WITHOUT A TELESCOPE

(COMET)

Named after Edmond Halley, who discovered that comets can show up more than once!

FIRST RECORDED IN 240 BCE

WE SEE IT EVERY 75-76 YEARS

IT'S BIG! MORE THAN 6 MILES IN DIAMETER

WILL PASS AGAIN IN 2061

IT WAS VISIBLE FROM EARTH ON THE YEAR MARK TWAIN WAS BORN AND THE YEAR HE DIED.

Before it passed by in 1910, some people were worried that the gas from the comet could kill everyone on Earth! People bought gas masks and even pills that claimed they could protect against comet gas.

All over the world people were even putting tape over their keyholes so that none of the vapors could get in. Of course, all of the hubbub was for nothing! The comet passing by was totally harmless.

ANTI-COMET PILLS

PART FIVE

SPACE

EXPLORATION

SCIENTISTS WHO LOOK AT THE SKY AND STUDY THE **STARS, PLANETS,** AND THE UNIVERSE ARE CALLED

ASTRONOMERS.

EARLY ASTRONOMERS

ERATOSTHENES (276-194 BCE)

In 200 BCE, this early astronomer used measurements based on the position of the stars to calculate the size of Earth. And centuries later when accurate measurements could be made, it turned out that he was only 211 miles off! The circumference of Earth is 24,901 miles.

THAT'S **REALLY** CLOSE! ESPECIALLY DURING AN ERA WHEN MOST PEOPLE STILL BELIEVED THAT THE EARTH WAS FLAT!

NICOLAUS COPERNICUS

1473-1543

This Polish astronomer came up with the idea that Earth revolved around the Sun. Before that, the commonly held belief was that Earth was the center of the universe.

GALILEO GALILEI

(1564-1642)

He discovered the moons of Jupiter and the rings of Saturn. He also created one of the first telescopes! He didn't invent the telescope, but he is credited with being the first person to use one for astronomy.

Galileo believed that Copernicus's theory was correct, and that Earth revolves around the Sun. Galileo's work got the attention of the leaders of the Catholic Church, who were firm believers that Earth was the center of the universe. They said that he wasn't allowed to talk about his findings publicly. But he didn't listen to them! After he published a new book saying that Copernicus was right, he was placed under house arrest for the rest of his life.

SIR ISAAC NEWTON

(1642-1727)

OUCH!

In 1668, Isaac Newton built the first reflecting telescope, which helped make telescopes more powerful and smaller. He also helped us understand gravity and how it influences the planets and their orbit. He also invented calculus!

Newton's first draft of the theory of gravity was accidentally destroyed in a fire . . . by a Pomeranian! The dog knocked over a candle, and the manuscript was destroyed. It took Newton a year to rewrite it.

OOPS!

VERA RUBIN

1928 - 2016

The astronomer who helped discover that the Universe is mostly made up of INVISIBLE DARK MATTER!

STEPHEN HAWKING

1942 - 2018

A scientist who is best known for his work explaining the origins of the universe and BLACK HOLES!

NANCY GRACE ROMAN

1925 - 2018

She created the space astronomy program at NASA and is often called the "Mother of Hubble" for all of the work she put into planning the Hubble Space Telescope.

NEIL de GRASSE TYSON

1958 - PRESENT

A scientist who has made it his goal to make science accessible. He's the director of the Hayden Planetarium, and he's an astrophysicist (which is the area of science that deals with the life and death of stars and other celestial objects).

TELESCOPES

OBJECTIVE LENS

Telescopes are really important tools for astronomers. They detect planets and other faraway objects. They do this by using curved lenses or mirrors to gather light into a smaller point.

FINDERSCOPE

OPTICAL TUBE

OPTICAL TUBE

We aren't exactly sure who invented the very first telescope, but the first person to apply for a patent for a telescope was a Dutch eyeglass maker named Hans Lipperhey.

MOUNT

Telescopes can be small enough to fit in your hand, but some are HUGE!

There's an extremely large telescope being built in Chile called the ELT. Want to know what that stands for? Extremely Large Telescope! When it's complete, it will be the most powerful land telescope ever.

HUBBLE SPACE TELESCOPE

THE EARTH'S ATMOSPHERE CAN OBSTRUCT OUR VIEW, SO THIS MASSIVE TELESCOPE WAS CREATED AND LAUNCHED INTO SPACE.

It's an optical telescope that is out in orbit. It can get clearer pictures than telescopes on Earth because it doesn't have interference from Earth's atmosphere.

Named after the astronomer Edwin P. Hubble, who found definitive evidence that there are other galaxies outside of the Milky Way

HAS MADE MILLIONS OF OBSERVATIONS SINCE IT LAUNCHED

POWERED BY SOLAR PANELS

43.5 FEET LONG

(about the length of a school bus)

LAUNCHED IN 1990

COST 2.5 BILLION DOLLARS

A BLURRY FIRST LOOK

Its first pictures weren't as clear as scientists had hoped. It turns out there was an incredibly small problem with the way one of the mirrors was made. Its shape was only off about the thickness of 1/50th of a sheet of paper... but that was still enough to make the telescope not work the way it should. Three years later, NASA launched a mission that fixed it. Since then, we've received some amazing photos from the Hubble.

JAMES WEBB SPACE TELESCOPE

It will be put into orbit 940,000 miles from Earth.

HAS A MIRROR COVERED WITH A THIN LAYER OF GOLD!

I know this looks like a space fighter jet, right? Well, it's actually a new, incredibly powerful telescope that's scheduled to launch into orbit in 2021.

It's estimated that it will be powerful enough that it could clearly read a penny from 24 miles away. It could detect the heat of a bumblebee that was as far away as the Moon!

It will fold up to fit inside the rocket that takes it into space and will unfold once it has been delivered.

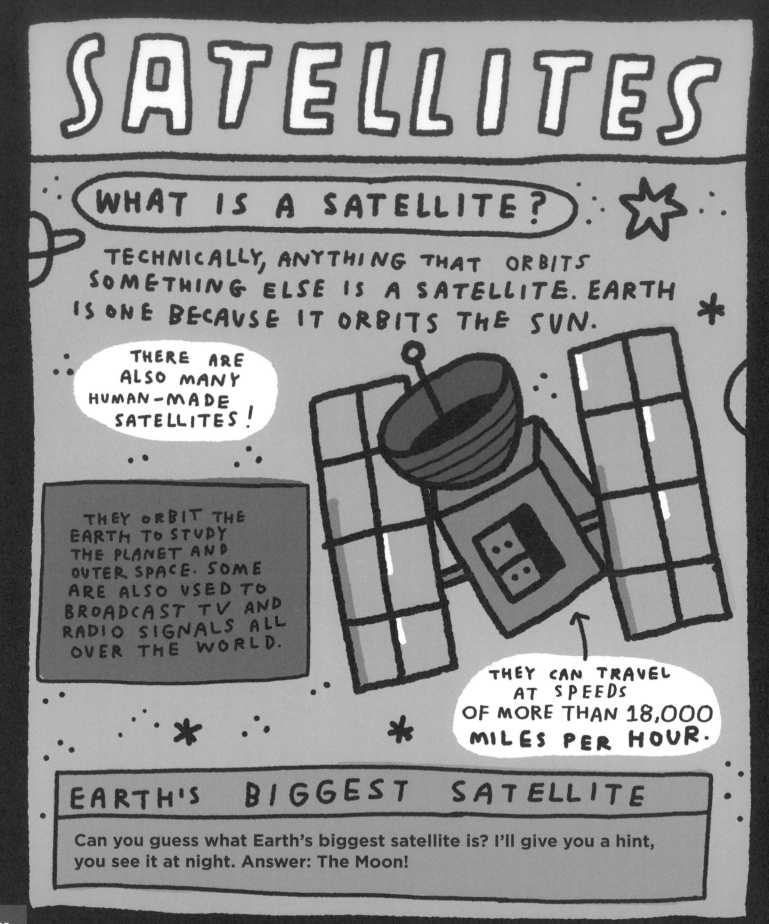

SATELLITES

WHAT IS A SATELLITE?

TECHNICALLY, ANYTHING THAT ORBITS SOMETHING ELSE IS A SATELLITE. EARTH IS ONE BECAUSE IT ORBITS THE SUN.

THERE ARE ALSO MANY HUMAN-MADE SATELLITES!

THEY ORBIT THE EARTH TO STUDY THE PLANET AND OUTER SPACE. SOME ARE ALSO USED TO BROADCAST TV AND RADIO SIGNALS ALL OVER THE WORLD.

THEY CAN TRAVEL AT SPEEDS OF MORE THAN 18,000 MILES PER HOUR.

EARTH'S BIGGEST SATELLITE

Can you guess what Earth's biggest satellite is? I'll give you a hint, you see it at night. Answer: The Moon!

THE DAWN OF THE SPACE AGE!

SPUTNIK СПУ́ТНИК

BEEP BEEP BEEP BEEP

In 1957, the Soviets launched a little, beach-ball-sized satellite into space. It was called Sputnik and it started the international space race between the US and the USSR. Both were trying to show off by being the first ones into space.

- ITS SIGNAL COULD BE PICKED UP AT HOME WITH SPECIAL RADIOS.

- SPUTNIK MEANS "SATELLITE" OR "TRAVELING COMPANION."

IT ORBITED EARTH FOR THREE WEEKS.

If you're not familiar with the USSR, don't try and look it up on the map. In 1922, Russia and a few surrounding countries joined and created one HUGE country, the USSR (Union of Soviet Socialist Republics). For a while it was the largest country in the world, but it disbanded in 1991. Now the biggest country in the world is Russia.

CCCP

IN 1961, YURI GAGARIN

FIRST HUMAN IN SPACE

became the first person to leave Earth's orbit, and fly into space! He orbited Earth once in the Vostok spacecraft for 108 minutes. The Vostok had no engines to help it slow down on the way back, so Yuri ejected 4 miles above Earth. Technically for the mission to be considered a spaceflight, the pilot was supposed to land with the vehicle . . . so the USSR just decided to leave out the part of the trip where he ejected.

SIDE FACT Yuri Gagarin died in 1968 in a jet fighter accident. When NASA's Apollo 11 mission landed on the Moon, they left behind a medallion with his name on it.

FIRST WOMAN IN SPACE!

COSMONAUT VALENTINA TERESHKOVA

Spent three days in orbit in 1963

FIRST AMERICAN IN SPACE!

JOHN GLENN

In 1962, John Glenn became the first NASA astronaut to orbit Earth. He went around Earth three times.

Later, in 1998, he went back to space, and at seventy-seven years old became the oldest person ever to space travel.

APOLLO 11: THE MISSION TO THE MOON!

IN 1969, THE US LAUNCHED A SPACE MISSION THAT SUCCESSFULLY PUT HUMANS ON THE MOON!

NASA

NASA (National Aeronautics and Space Administration) is a department of the United States government that focuses on space programs and research. It was founded in 1958.

APOLLO 11 LUNAR MODULE

(AKA EAGLE) THIS WAS THE FIRST CREWED VEHICLE TO LAND ON THE MOON.

COMMAND MODULE COLUMBIA

NEIL ARMSTRONG

FIRST PERSON ON THE MOON!

In 1969, four days after takeoff, Neil stepped on the Moon's surface, and said the now iconic words:

THAT'S ONE SMALL STEP FOR MAN, ONE GIANT LEAP FOR MANKIND.

TOOK FLYING LESSONS <u>BEFORE</u> HE HAD A DRIVER'S LICENSE.

He took most of the photos during the first moonwalk, so most of the pictures are of Buzz, not Neil.

Well, at least that's what we heard back here on Earth! What he actually said was "That's one small step for A man, one giant leap for mankind." The "A" before "man" got lost in transmission.

EDWIN "BUZZ" ALDRIN

HE WAS THE SECOND PERSON ON THE MOON!

He gets a weird award: First person to use the bathroom on the Moon award! It's true! Okay, maybe it was in his suit (it's designed to collect waste), but it still counts! Right?

MICHAEL COLLINS

He's not as well known as the other guys on the mission, but Michael's role was very important. He piloted the command module around the far side of the Moon while Neil and Buzz were on their 22-hour mission.

600 MILLION PEOPLE WATCHED THE FIRST MOON WALK. IT WAS THE LARGEST TV AUDIENCE IN HISTORY AT THE TIME.

IT'S ESTIMATED THAT IT TOOK AROUND 400,000 SCIENTISTS, ENGINEERS, AND OTHER PEOPLE TO MAKE THE MOON LANDING POSSIBLE.

OOPS... I FORGOT MY KEYS.

THERE WAS NO OUTER HANDLE ON THE MODULE THAT LANDED ON THE MOON. WHICH MEANS THAT THERE WAS A CHANCE THEY COULD HAVE LOCKED THEMSELVES OUT!

IT WAS A STINKY RIDE!

Apollo 11 had a little problem with its drinking water... it was accidentally really bubbly! This resulted in some zero-gravity gas for the astronauts.

PIECES OF THE WRIGHT BROTHERS' FIRST AIRPLANE WERE ON BOARD.

A MODERN CELL PHONE IS WAAAY SMARTER THAN THE APOLLO **11** COMPUTERS.

THE FOOTPRINTS ON THE MOON LEFT BY THE ASTRONAUTS COULD BE THERE FOR A REALLY LONG TIME.

Since there's no wind or water to erode them away, they could just stay there. Unless the Moon was hit by a meteorite close to where the footprints are.

The astronauts had to be quarantined for 18 days after landing, because scientists were worried they may have brought back microbes from the Moon.

HUMAN COMPUTERS

Even though the first men in space got all the attention, it took thousands of scientists and other workers to get the rocket off the ground. This included a group of incredibly important, behind-the-scenes women who made the mission possible. They were called the West Area Computers, and were a group of Black mathematicians who made the calculations of possible trajectories for the rocket.

KATHERINE JOHNSON

One of the human computers, she worked at NASA for over 35 years, and her calculations were critical for the success of space missions.

IN 2015, SHE RECEIVED THE PRESIDENTIAL MEDAL OF FREEDOM FROM PRESIDENT BARACK OBAMA.

SATURN V ROCKET

SATURN V (FIVE) WAS THE TYPE OF ROCKET THAT TOOK THE FIRST MEN TO THE MOON.

363 FEET TALL!

The rocket was so heavy that the transporter that carried it to the launchpad could only go 1 mile per hour! That's slower than an iceberg typically moves!

MORE POWERFUL THAN **30** JUMBO JETS!

Saturn V rockets made other missions and took twenty-four men to the Moon.

COULD TRAVEL MORE THAN 25,000 MILES PER HOUR!

CRAZY FACT!

THE WRIGHT BROTHERS

THERE WERE ONLY 65 YEARS BETWEEN THE VERY FIRST FLIGHT AND THE MOON LANDING.

UNITED STATES

USA USA

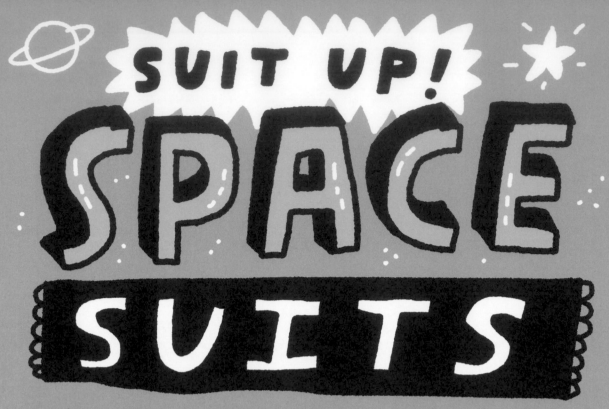

SUIT UP! SPACE SUITS

SO, YOU WANT TO GO TO SPACE? WELL, DON'T FORGET YOUR SUIT! HUMANS WOULDN'T BE ABLE TO SURVIVE IN SPACE WITHOUT PROTECTION.

YOU'D ONLY SURVIVE FOR ABOUT FIFTEEN SECONDS!

WHAT WOULD HAPPEN TO YOU IN SPACE WITHOUT A SPACE SUIT?

You would freeze!

There's no oxygen, so you wouldn't be able to breathe!

Your entire body would inflate like a balloon due to pressure!

Your skin would get burned from the Sun's radiation!

You could get hit at high speeds by micrometeoroids (little rocks) or debris from spacecraft!

When you're in space, it's important to keep your cool! Astronauts wear a special cooling mechanism under their suit that helps them stay cool inside all of that gear. There are vents to draw away sweat, and tubes that cycle cold water near their skin.

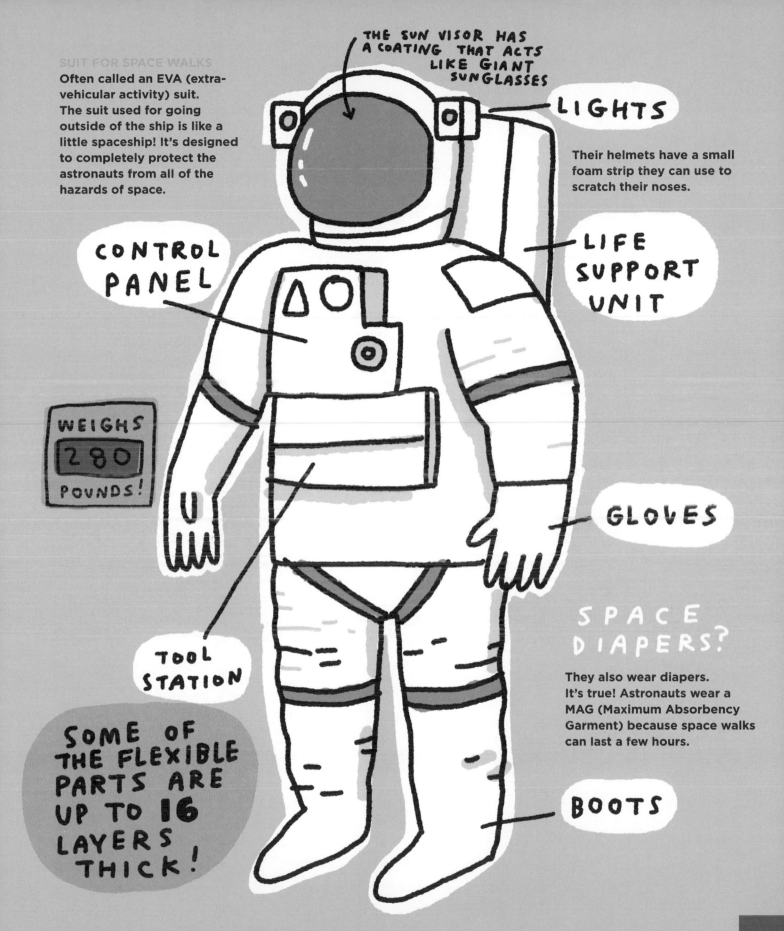

THE SUN VISOR HAS A COATING THAT ACTS LIKE GIANT SUNGLASSES

Often called an EVA (extra-vehicular activity) suit. The suit used for going outside of the ship is like a little spaceship! It's designed to completely protect the astronauts from all of the hazards of space.

LIGHTS

Their helmets have a small foam strip they can use to scratch their noses.

CONTROL PANEL

LIFE SUPPORT UNIT

WEIGHS 280 POUNDS!

GLOVES

TOOL STATION

SPACE DIAPERS?

They also wear diapers. It's true! Astronauts wear a MAG (Maximum Absorbency Garment) because space walks can last a few hours.

SOME OF THE FLEXIBLE PARTS ARE UP TO 16 LAYERS THICK!

BOOTS

*HOW TO BE AN ASTRONAUT

(DO YOU HAVE WHAT IT TAKES ?!)

NASA'S REQUIREMENTS

① YOU MUST ★ A US CITIZEN. ★

③ YOU MUST HAVE A MASTER'S DEGREE IN A STEM FIELD, INCLUDING ENGINEERING, BIOLOGICAL SCIENCE, PHYSICAL SCIENCE, COMPUTER SCIENCE OR MATHEMATICS.

② YOU MUST HAVE 1,000 HOURS OF EXPERIENCE AS PILOT-IN-COMMAND TIME ON JET AIRCRAFT <u>OR</u> TWO YEARS OF RELATED PROFESSIONAL EXPERIENCE.

④ YOU MUST PASS THE NASA ASTRONAUT PHYSICAL.

YOU MUST ALSO BE SKILLED IN LEADERSHIP, TEAMWORK, AND COMMUNICATION.

NASA RECEIVED MORE THAN **18,000** ASTRONAUT APPLICATIONS IN 2019.

ONCE SELECTED, YOU MUST GO TO ASTRONAUT SCHOOL! THERE YOU WILL LEARN SKILLS LIKE SPACE WALKING, WORKING IN A SPACE STATION, AND CONTROLLING A ROBOTIC ARM!

MY FINGERS ARE REALLY WRINKLY NOW.

ASTRONAUTS TRAIN UNDERWATER IN A POOL FOR UP TO **7 HOURS!**

Floating in a pool is a lot like floating around in zero gravity. The Neutral Buoyancy Laboratory (the pool where they train) is 202 feet wide, 102 feet long, and 40 feet deep. It's filled with 6.2 million gallons of water.

Astronauts have to swim laps with their 250-pound flight suits and shoes on.

TAKE A RIDE ON THE **VOMIT COMET!**

BEING AN ASTRONAUT HAS ITS UPS AND DOWNS!

Another part of the training for an astronaut is to take a reduced-gravity ride in a jet here on Earth. The jet climbs at a 45 degree angle, and then falls at the same angle quickly. This creates around 25 seconds of simulated weightlessness. A typical training session would go through this process 40–60 times.

It's estimated that one third of the passengers get really airsick from this, one third just get kind of sick, and one third are okay with it.

THE INTERNATIONAL SPACE STATION (ISS)

It has six areas for sleeping, two bathrooms, and even a gym. Astronauts have to work out at least two hours a day because microgravity leads to muscle loss.

IT'S 357 FEET LONG!

That's about the size of a football field!

It's estimated that it cost around

$120 BILLION

to build, making it the most expensive object ever built!

Every astronaut who goes to the International Space Station must learn to speak RUSSIAN.

Привет!

It's 248 miles above Earth.

(42 times higher than what a typical airplane would fly!)

It circles the globe every 90 minutes. So every day, the astronauts aboard the ISS see sixteen sunrises and sunsets.

AS OF 2020, 239 PEOPLE HAVE VISITED ISS FROM 19 COUNTRIES.

It's been occupied since November 2000.

IT'S THE LARGEST HUMAN-MADE THING IN SPACE.

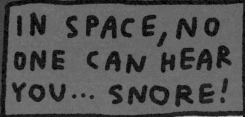

IN SPACE, NO ONE CAN HEAR YOU... SNORE!

BECAUSE THERE'S NO GRAVITY PUSHING ON YOUR WINDPIPE, THERE'S NO SNORING!

FOOD iN SPACE!

EARLY SPACE FOOD CAME IN **TUBES** AND WAS SQUEEZED OUT LIKE **TOOTHPASTE.**

THE FIRST MEAL IN SPACE WAS A TUBE OF **BEEF** AND **LIVER** PASTE.

Other early space foods were freeze-dried. They were dehydrated, and sealed in airtight packaging. When astronauts were hungry they could open them with scissors and inject cold water to eat.

ANOTHER EARLY SPACE FOOD WAS A TUBE OF APPLESAUCE.

YUM!

TODAY, FOOD IN SPACE IS A **LOT** BETTER. ASTRONAUT MEALS ARE NO LONGER LIMITED TO WEIRD **TUBES.**

Cookies were the first food baked in space. But get this!

THE ASTRONAUTS DIDN'T GET TO EAT THEM

because they were part of an experiment. But, they did get to eat some pre-baked cookies that they brought with them.

If astronauts tried to use regular salt and pepper, it would be a real mess. It would just float away and could clog up air vents and get in their eyes. So, astronauts use liquid salt and pepper.

AN ASTRONAUT ONCE SNUCK A CORNED-BEEF SANDWICH ONTO A FLIGHT. (HE GOT INTO BIG TROUBLE.)

SPACE TACOS

Astronauts like to make sandwiches with tortillas. They're great because they don't crumble like regular bread and they're flat and easy to store.

A FEW OTHER THINGS THAT HAVE BEEN EATEN IN SPACE

STRAWBERRY CEREAL

FRUIT CAKE

SHRIMP

BORSCHT (BEET SOUP!)

CRUNCHY ICE CREAM!?

NASA has been trying to make better-tasting foods for the astronauts so, of course, they had to make everyone's favorite frosty treat, **ICE CREAM**! To make it edible in space, they freeze-dried it, which means it doesn't need to be refrigerated. It also takes all of the water out of it and makes it crunchy. It's still sold today in museum gift shops as **SPACE FOOD**... but it's never actually been served in space. NASA decided it would crumble too easily.

ROVERS

Rovers are supersmart, uncrewed vehicles that have been sent to explore other planets and the Moon. They are remotely controlled from Earth, but are also programmed to automatically complete tasks on their own.

They help us analyze the soil and atmosphere, make measurements, and take lots of photographs.

HAS A 7-FOOT-LONG ARM

Part of NASA's **Mars Science Laboratory (MSL)** mission

EXPLORED **MARS** FOR 3 YEARS

FIRST VEHICLE WITH WHEELS TO LAND ON ANOTHER PLANET

SOJOURNER

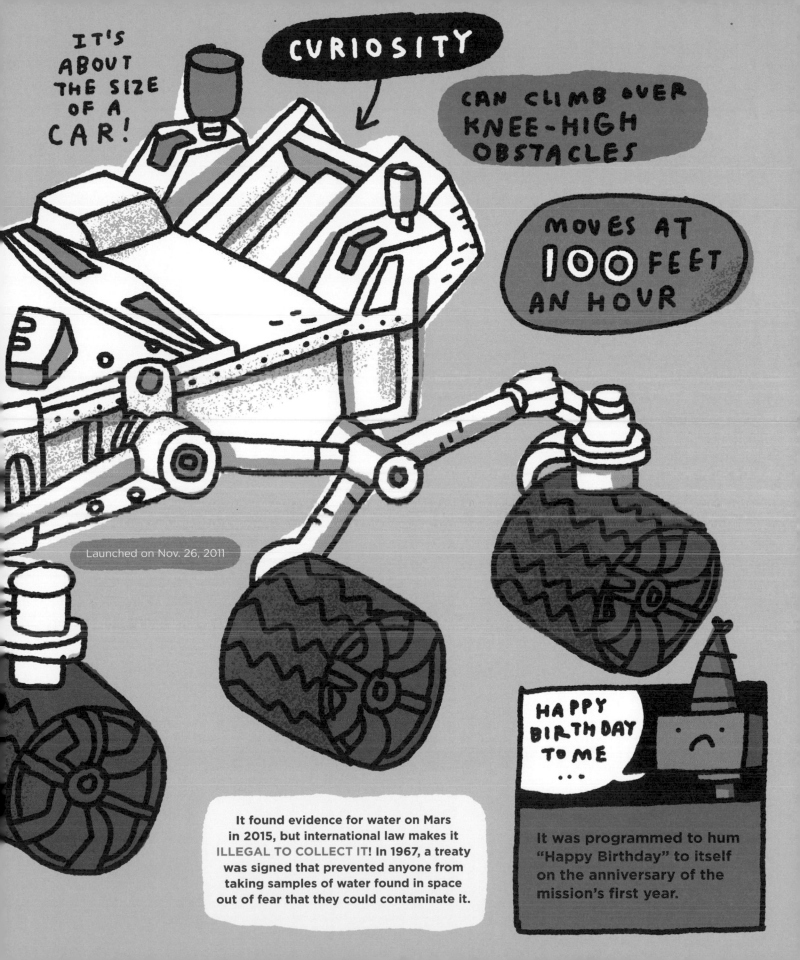

It found evidence for water on Mars in 2015, but international law makes it ILLEGAL TO COLLECT IT! In 1967, a treaty was signed that prevented anyone from taking samples of water found in space out of fear that they could contaminate it.

It was programmed to hum "Happy Birthday" to itself on the anniversary of the mission's first year.

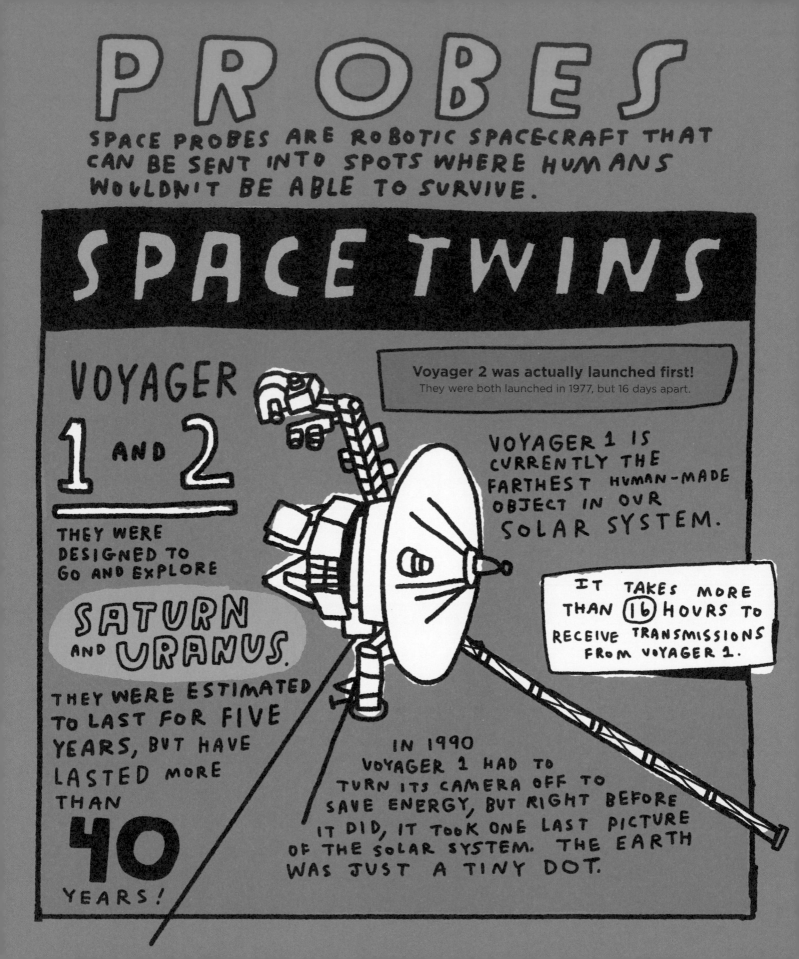

PROBES

SPACE PROBES ARE ROBOTIC SPACECRAFT THAT CAN BE SENT INTO SPOTS WHERE HUMANS WOULDN'T BE ABLE TO SURVIVE.

SPACE TWINS

VOYAGER 1 AND 2

THEY WERE DESIGNED TO GO AND EXPLORE **SATURN AND URANUS.**

THEY WERE ESTIMATED TO LAST FOR FIVE YEARS, BUT HAVE LASTED MORE THAN **40** YEARS!

Voyager 2 was actually launched first!
They were both launched in 1977, but 16 days apart.

VOYAGER 1 IS CURRENTLY THE FARTHEST HUMAN-MADE OBJECT IN OUR SOLAR SYSTEM.

IT TAKES MORE THAN (16) HOURS TO RECEIVE TRANSMISSIONS FROM VOYAGER 1.

IN 1990 VOYAGER 1 HAD TO TURN ITS CAMERA OFF TO SAVE ENERGY, BUT RIGHT BEFORE IT DID, IT TOOK ONE LAST PICTURE OF THE SOLAR SYSTEM. THE EARTH WAS JUST A TINY DOT.

IT'S A MESSAGE FOR ANY INTELLIGENT LIFE THAT MIGHT FIND IT.

IT'S FULL OF SOUNDS AND IMAGES FROM EARTH.

(IF SOMEONE FINDS IT, THEY WOULD JUST HAVE TO FIGURE OUT HOW TO PLAY A RECORD.)

SOUNDS INCLUDED ON THE RECORD INCLUDE

THUNDER | CLASSICAL MUSIC | "JOHNNY B. GOOD" | INTERNATIONAL GREETINGS

¡HOLA! NI HAO! BONJOUR! SALVE! OLÁ! NAMASTE!

WILD DOG | FOOTSTEPS | FIRE | FROGS

VOYAGER 1 IS HEADED TOWARD A STAR CALLED AC +79 3888.
IN 40,000 YEARS IT WILL BE WITHIN 1.7 LIGHT YEARS OF IT!

SPACE SHUTTLE

THE SPACE SHUTTLE PROGRAM LASTED FROM THE 1980s TO 2011. SPACE SHUTTLES WERE THE FIRST REUSABLE SPACECRAFT AND COULD CARRY CREWS OF 2-7 ASTRONAUTS.

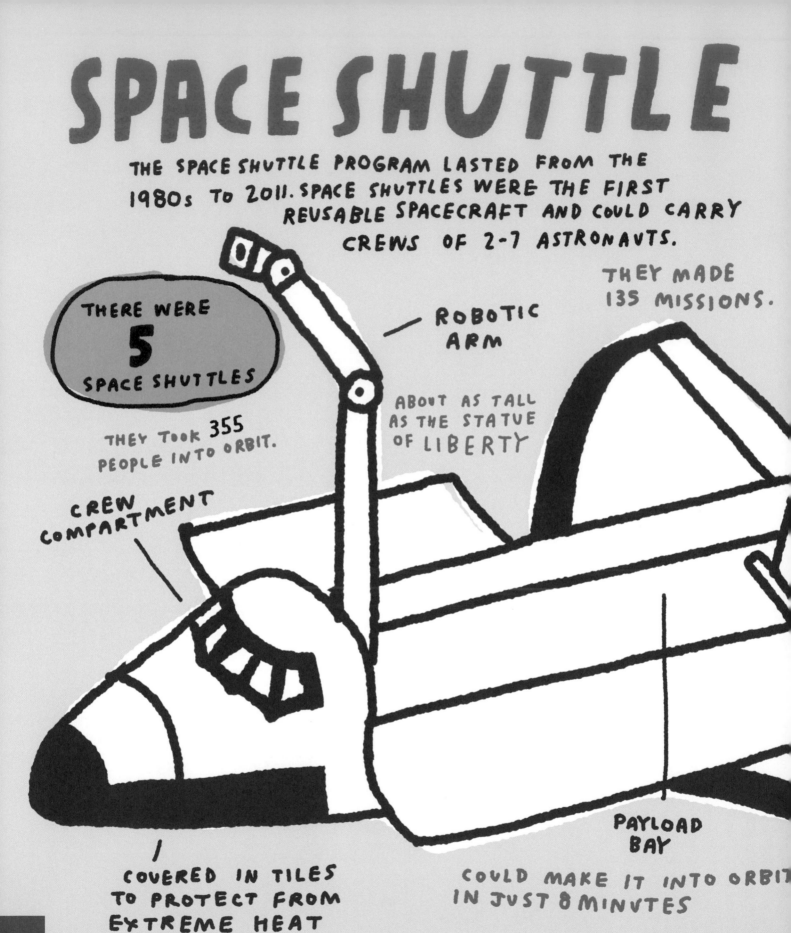

THERE WERE **5** SPACE SHUTTLES

ROBOTIC ARM

THEY MADE 135 MISSIONS.

THEY TOOK 355 PEOPLE INTO ORBIT.

ABOUT AS TALL AS THE STATUE OF LIBERTY

CREW COMPARTMENT

COVERED IN TILES TO PROTECT FROM EXTREME HEAT

PAYLOAD BAY

COULD MAKE IT INTO ORBIT IN JUST 8 MINUTES

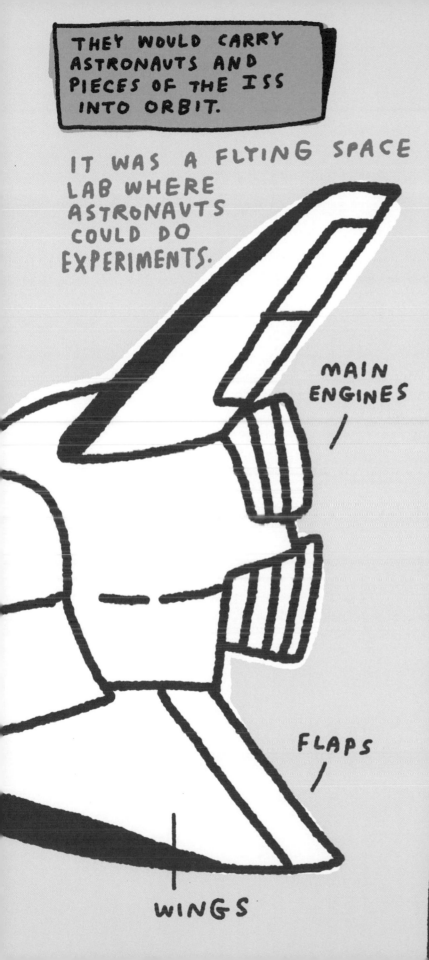

THEY WOULD CARRY ASTRONAUTS AND PIECES OF THE ISS INTO ORBIT.

IT WAS A FLYING SPACE LAB WHERE ASTRONAUTS COULD DO EXPERIMENTS.

MAIN ENGINES

FLAPS

WINGS

USA

SPACE SHUTTLES WOULD LAUNCH INTO SPACE ON THESE HUGE ROCKETS THAT WOULD FALL AWAY ONCE THE SHUTTLE WAS IN ORBIT. IT TRAVELED AT 17,000 MILES PER HOUR!

SPACEX

IN 2011, NASA RETIRED ITS SERVICE OF TRANSPORTING ASTRONAUTS TO THE SPACE STATION, AND SOME COMPANIES HAVE STARTED BUILDING THEIR OWN

ROCKET SHIPS!

FLYING CARS?!

ONE OF SPACEX'S FIRST DELIVERIES WAS A RED TESLA SPORTS CAR.

IT'S DRIVEN BY A DUMMY! YOU CAN SEE FOOTAGE OF IT FLOATING THROUGH SPACE ONLINE.

HE'S CALLED "STARMAN."

FOUNDED BY BILLIONAIRE ELON MUSK, WHO IS ALSO THE FOUNDER OF TESLA, INC., A COMPANY THAT MAKES ELECTRIC CARS

SPACEX WAS THE FIRST PRIVATE COMPANY TO LAUNCH A SPACECRAFT THAT CIRCLED THE EARTH.

FALCON HEAVY

IT'S THE MOST POWERFUL ROCKET EVER!

IT'S AT LEAST 2 TIMES MORE POWERFUL THAN ANY OTHER SPACECRAFT!

IT CAN DELIVER SATELLITES INTO ORBIT.

IT USES THE SAME LAUNCHPAD AT THE KENNEDY SPACE CENTER THAT NASA USES.

WEIRD FACT!

The SpaceX rocket, the Falcon 9, took the cremated remains of James Doohan (who played Scotty on *Star Trek*) into space.

There's even a company that will take your ashes into space for as little as around $2,500.

ANIMALS IN SPACE!

HUMANS AREN'T THE ONLY LIVING THINGS THAT HAVE BEEN TO SPACE. HERE ARE A FEW OTHER ASTRONAUT CREATURES.

FRUIT FLIES

1ST ANIMAL IN SPACE

(1947)

Yep, that's right! Way before Neil Armstrong took his famous steps on the Moon, some fruit flies were the very first living things to ever go into space. In 1947, they rode aboard a V-2 rocket that launched them 68 miles into the sky.

WHY FRUIT FLIES?!

Humans weren't sent initially because scientists were worried that cosmic radiation would be harmful. And it turns out a fruit fly's genetic code is more similar to ours than you might think! So, what was the result? The flies weren't harmed and their trip opened the door for humans to eventually make their way into space.

MOUSE (1957)

CAT (1963)

LOTS OF MONKEYS (THE FIRST ONE WAS IN 1949.)

MEALWORMS (1968)

RABBIT (1959)

LAIKA (1957)

The first living thing ever in orbit was Laika, a dog from Russia.

ALSO: JELLYFISH

SPIDERS

FISH

FROGS

FIRST LIVING THING TO SURVIVE IN SPACE WITHOUT A SPACE SUIT

IN 2011, THESE MICROSCOPIC ANIMALS WERE PUT OUTSIDE OF A SPACESHIP FOR TEN DAYS AND THEN BROUGHT BACK TO EARTH. 68% OF THEM SURVIVED.

TARDIGRADES

(SOMETIMES CALLED "WATER BEARS")

THEY ARE CONSIDERED TO BE THE MOST RESILIENT ANIMALS EVER DISCOVERED.

WHICH MEANS THEY CAN HANDLE INCREDIBLY HARSH CONDITIONS LIKE THOSE FOUND IN SPACE.

THEY CAN LIVE UP TO 30 YEARS WITHOUT FOOD AND WATER!

EVERYDAY STUFF THAT WE HAVE BECAUSE OF SPACE RESEARCH

Here are just a few of the things that we use every single day that are the result of research done for space travel and exploration!

PROSTHETIC LIMBS

SCRATCH-RESISTANT LENSES

TINY CAMERAS IN PHONES

SOLAR PANELS

WATER FILTRATION

BABY FORMULA

BEFORE AFTER

CORRECTIVE EYE SURGERY

AIR PURIFIERS

LED LIGHTS

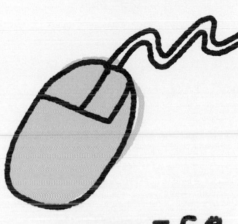

COMPUTER MOUSE

EAR THERMOMETER

PORTABLE COMPUTERS

MINI VACUUMS

As the technology used in the space shuttles started to age, some of the components became harder to find. So much so that at one point they actually had to search for some ... ON EBAY!

DISPLAY

E3

NOT A LASER GUN!

TRIGGER

POWER SUPPLY

ASTRONAUTS USE A SPECIAL TOOL CALLED A **PGT** THAT CAN DO LOTS OF STUFF.
(PGT stands for pistol-grip tool.)

They've been used by astronauts on the ISS and while working on the Hubble Telescope.

Can withstand a 500-degree temperature change!

IN 2006 AN ASTRONAUT ACCIDENTALLY DROPPED A SPATULA WHILE ON A SPACE WALK!

No, he wasn't out there making scrambled eggs! He was using it to test some heat tiles. It later burned up when reentering Earth's atmosphere.

ASTRONAUTS ARE WOKEN UP BY SONGS PLAYED FROM MISSION CONTROL BACK ON EARTH. THEY EVEN GET TO CHOOSE THE SONG FOR THEIR ALARM CLOCK!

(Some real examples are "Rocket Man" by Elton John and "Space Oddity" by David Bowie)

♫ ROCKET MAAN! ♫

FUTURE EXPLORATION

The first rocket was launched into space less than 100 years ago. Since then, hundreds of humans have been to space. In that time there have been hundreds of missions, and today we have a multi-billion-dollar space station.

We've made more discoveries in that time than we ever thought could be possible. What does that mean for future space exploration?

What will we accomplish in the next 100 years?

What about the next 1,000 years?

Will we find new technology to help us reach faraway planets?

Will we ever encounter intelligent life from

OUTER SPACE?

Only time will tell, but the following pages are a few of the planned and proposed space exploration projects.

PLANNED (AND PROPOSED) FUTURE SPACE PROJECTS AND MISSIONS

STUDYING THE DEPTHS OF THE OCEANS FROM SPACE

STUDYING THE KUIPER BELT

LOOKING FOR SIGNS OF LIFE ON ONE OF JUPITER'S MOONS

BREAKTHROUGH STARSHOT

This project aims to reach Alpha Centauri star system in just 20 years. That may seem like a long time, but using the technology we currently use, it would take more than 30,000 years to get there! To do it, researchers will send incredibly small and light spacecraft (about the size of a stamp!) that will be propelled by small lasers beamed from Earth. Alpha Centauri is the closest planetary system to us!

DRAGONFLY

This spacecraft will be sent to Titan, the largest of Saturn's moons. Its mission is to study the surface to see if it's able to support early forms of life. It's a quadcopter, which means it has four propellers that help it get around.

LUNAR FLASHLIGHT
THIS SMALL SATELLITE WILL FLY OVER AREAS OF THE MOON THAT ARE ALWAYS DARK.
ABOUT THE SIZE OF A BRIEFCASE
IT WILL USE LASERS TO MAP THE ICE THERE.
ZAP!

WAIT!
WHAT ABOUT ALIENS?

IS THERE LIFE ON OTHER PLANETS?

THE SHORT ANSWER IS

↓

WE DON'T KNOW.

We've never found life on other planets.

NO ALIEN SIGHTINGS HAVE BEEN CONFIRMED TO BE TRUE!

As you now know, our universe is

HUGE!

It's impossibly big. And it's full of very hard-to-explain stuff like black holes and stars that are a lot bigger than ours. All that to say, we don't know what is out there.

HERE'S WHAT WE DO KNOW.

THE GOLDILOCKS ZONE!

STAR

TOO HOT

JUST RIGHT!

TOO COLD

To be hospitable to life, planets can't be too close or too far away from their suns, otherwise the climate would be too hot or too cold for liquid water—which living things need to survive! This is called the "Goldilocks Zone," which means it's "just right" to be hospitable to life.

But get this. Astronomers have already CONFIRMED a few planets that would meet those requirements!

One study suggests that there could be as many as

60 BILLION

planets in the universe that could support life!

There's an organization whose mission is to find and research alien life! They're called the SETI Institute. SETI stands for Search for Extra-Terrestrial Intelligence. One of the ways that they look for life on other planets is with large radio dishes that they point toward space in hopes of picking up alien radio signals. They also send radio signals out, but so far we've not gotten a response.

PART SIX

LET'S DRAW SPACE STUFF!

LET'S DRAW SPACE STUFF!

SUPPLIES:

You don't need fancy art supplies to draw space stuff! Here are a few things that I like to draw with, but you can use whatever you've got.

PENCIL

CRAYONS

NOTEBOOK PAPER →

MARKERS

SKETCHBOOK ↓

ZOOM

ZOOM

IMPORTANT!

It's important to know that your drawings will be significantly better if you make rocket sounds while making them. Especially if you are in a crowded, quiet area.

EARTH

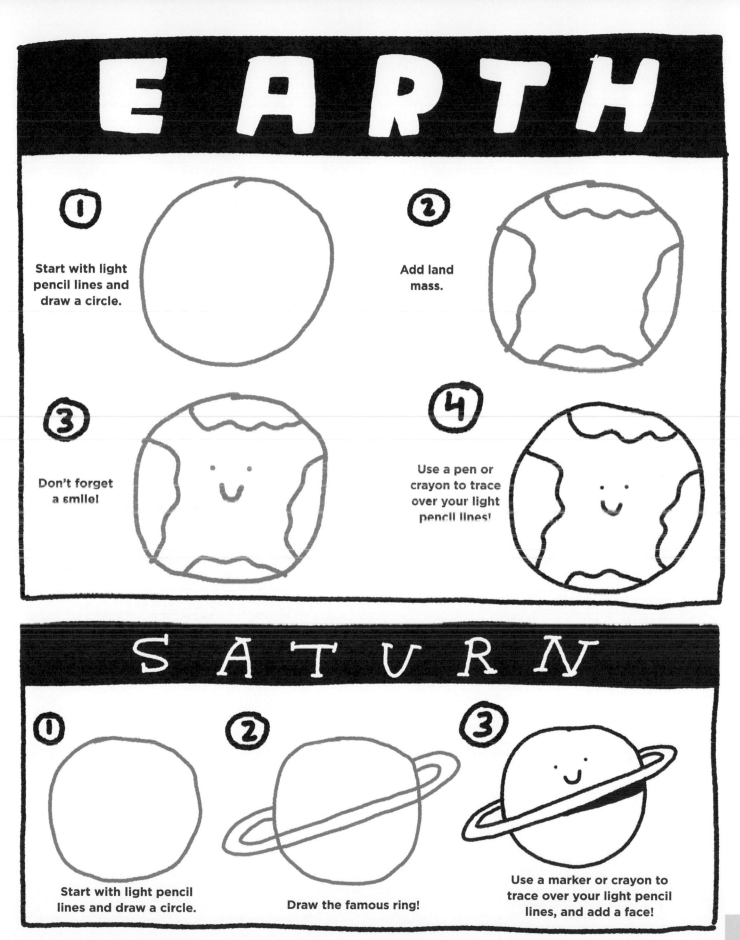

1 Start with light pencil lines and draw a circle.

2 Add land mass.

3 Don't forget a smile!

4 Use a pen or crayon to trace over your light pencil lines!

SATURN

1 Start with light pencil lines and draw a circle.

2 Draw the famous ring!

3 Use a marker or crayon to trace over your light pencil lines, and add a face!

ROCKET SHIP

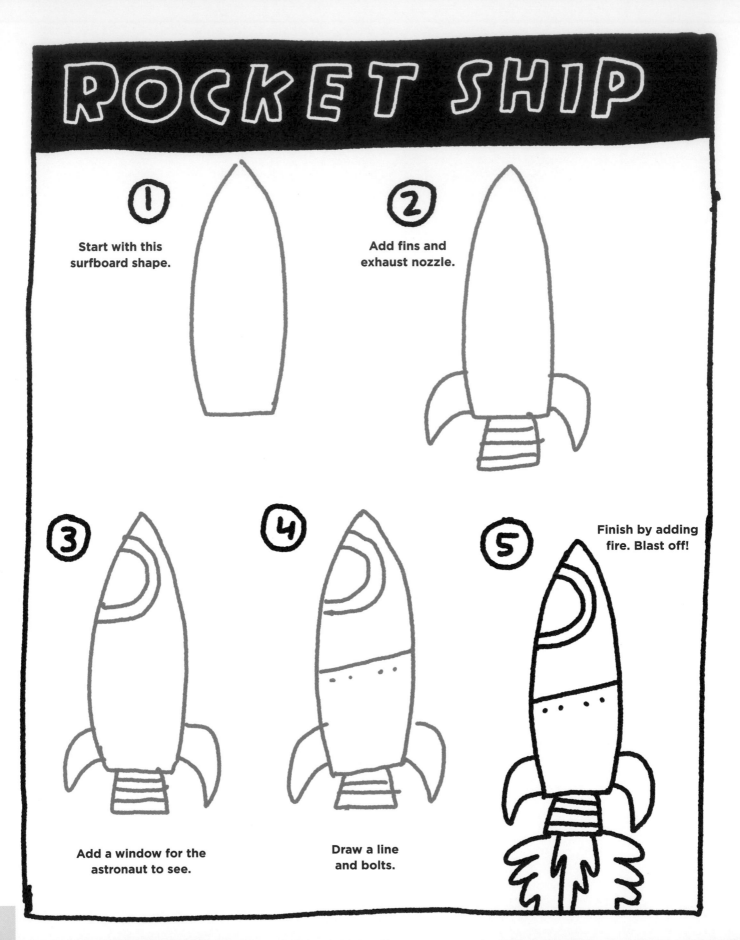

① Start with this surfboard shape.

② Add fins and exhaust nozzle.

③ Add a window for the astronaut to see.

④ Draw a line and bolts.

⑤ Finish by adding fire. Blast off!

ASTRONAUT

1 Start with the helmet.

2 Add the body and control panel.

3 Draw the arms and legs.

4 Finish by adding a connector tube!

U F O

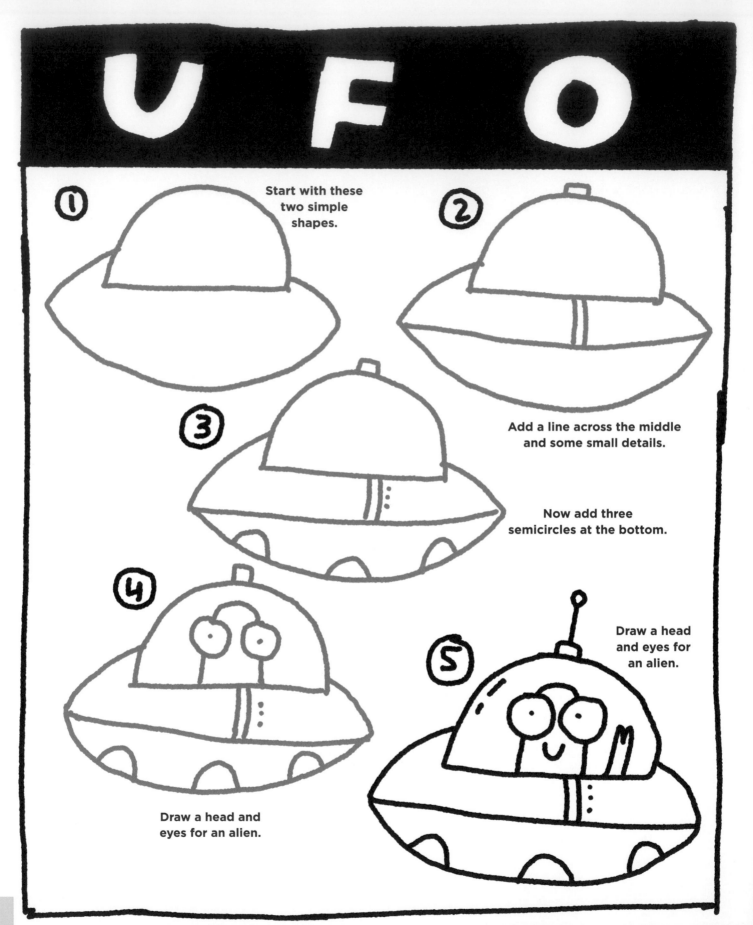

① Start with these two simple shapes.

② Add a line across the middle and some small details.

③ Now add three semicircles at the bottom.

④ Draw a head and eyes for an alien.

⑤ Draw a head and eyes for an alien.

SATELLITE

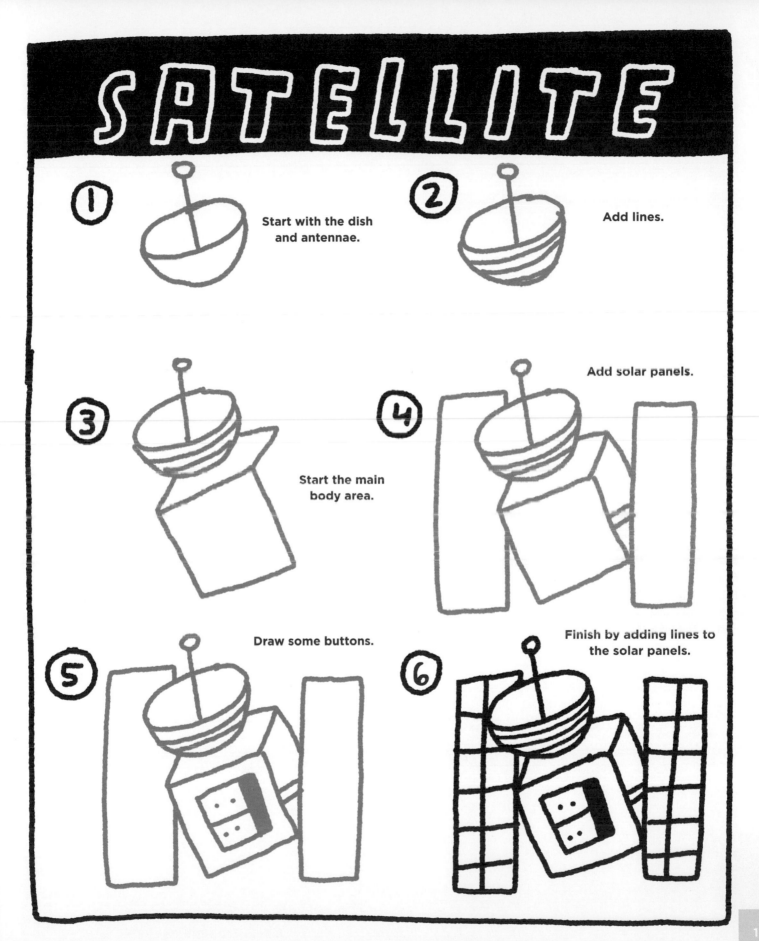

① Start with the dish and antennae.

② Add lines.

③ Start the main body area.

④ Add solar panels.

⑤ Draw some buttons.

⑥ Finish by adding lines to the solar panels.

SPACE JOKES

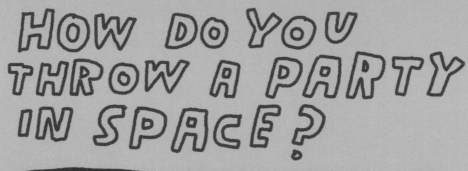
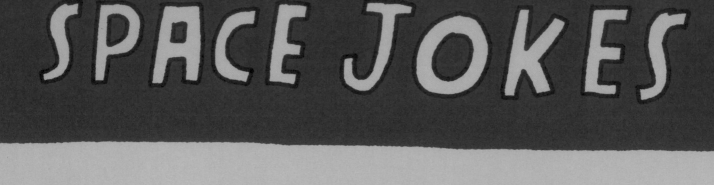

A few out-of-this-world resources I used while working on this book!

Dimwiddie, Robert. *The Planets: The Definitive Visual Guide to Our Solar System*. New York: DK Publishing, 2014.

DK Publishing. *Space!: The Universe as You've Never Seen It Before*. New York: DK Publishing, 2015.

Nelson, Craig. *Rocket Men: The Epic Story of the First Men on the Moon*. New York: Penguin Books, 2010.

Ridpath, Ian. *Stars and Planets: The Most Complete Guide to the Stars, Planets, Galaxies, and Solar System—Updated and Expanded Edition*. Princeton, New Jersey: Princeton University Press, 2017.

Shetterly, Margot Lee. *Hidden Figures: The American Dream and the Untold Story of the Black Women Mathematicians Who Helped Win the Space Race*. New York: HarperCollins Publishers, 2016.

Trefil, James. *Space Atlas, Second Edition: Mapping the Universe and Beyond*. Washington, DC: National Geographic, 2018.

NASA.gov. Digital. https://www.nasa.gov

Space. Digital. https://www.space.com